The vOUCHers Pack

Template letter for parents & carers

Children's Assembly Presentation

Staff 'How to' Presentation

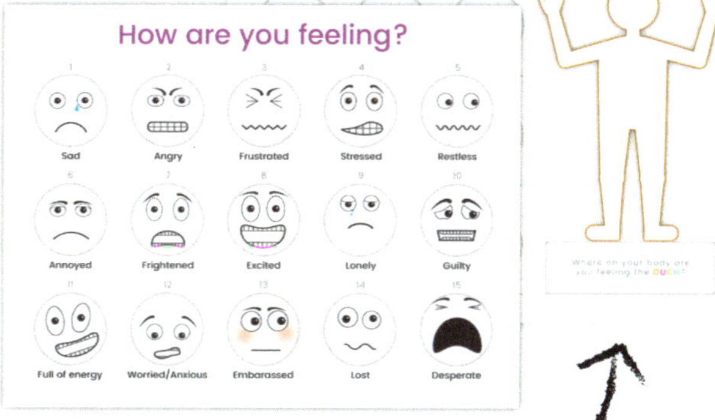

Laminated feelings pages

Symbol Exchange Cards

Learn more at www.OUCHer.net

vOUCHers book

School and Class Posters

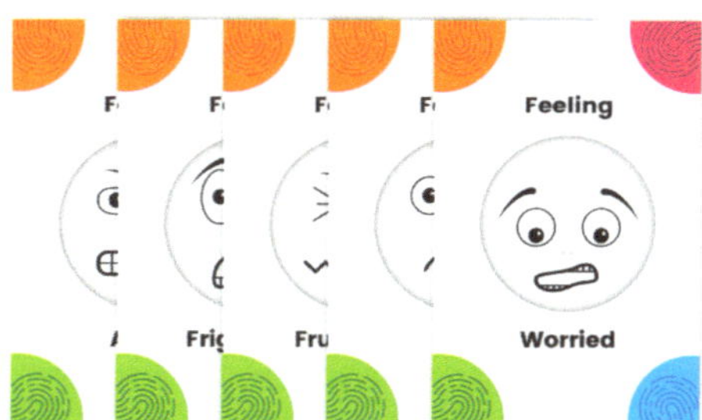

Learn more at www.OUCHer.net

Many thanks to all of those who helped us bring this project to life.
Cheri Blackamore BA (Hons), Former Secondary School Inclusion Manager
Jeanette Jameson, Headteacher, Quadring Cowley and Brown's Primary School
Kirsten Jones, Pastoral Coordinator, Sleaford Church Lane Primary School
Louise Curtis, Learning Mentor, St Nicholas CE Primary Academy part of Infinity Trust
Trish Hicken, Specialist Language Teacher & Team Leader for Extended Communication
and Language Impairment for Students (ECLIPS) team, Lincolnshire County Council.

The advice and information provided in this book is for general help and guidance only and anyone at all unsure of how to deal with a specific problem should consult an appropriate professional. We do our utmost to bring you relevant and reliable information, but we can take no responsibility for any advice offered.

The book is not, necessarily, endorsed or supported by any charities that appear in this book. Their names, brands and their logos are shown for your reference only.

This book has been created to share the work of the author(s) and has not been designed to be upsetting or offensive in any way.

vOUCHers
School Edition
Jennifer Dunning & Mark 'Markus' Baker

Published by R-and-Q.com.

ISBN: 978-1-9163571-5-0

vOUCHers

The idea stemmed from a conversation with one of the author's daughter. At the start of the 2020 March lockdown, Jennifer spent time talking through internet safety with her children, aged ten and seven, building upon their school's teaching. All seemed to go well for three weeks until one evening, as Jennifer was tucking her 10 year old into bed, her daughter announced that she had needed to tell her something. Her look was of fear, her words shaky.

"Go on, I am listening," said Jennifer.

"Mum, I went on a website I shouldn't have."
Jennifer gave her her silence and space to allow her to tell her more. She went on to explain that she had accidentally clicked on a pop up site. It transpired that it was an innocent site. No harm done.

"Are you mad at me, mum?" Her daughter asked.

The conversation continued and her daughter explained that it happened over a week ago and she had not had the courage to tell her mum, worried about what she would say: "I was afraid to tell you because you'd told us the rules of being online and I broke them. I thought you'd be angry."

This led onto Jennifer to think, if her own daughter held this worry inside her and, in fact, a very innocent fear from an action that in this instance led her to no danger, what of other children who have similar secrets, or indeed secrets of a grander, more serious scale. Potentially of trauma, fear and real danger, but not have anyone to tell.

Following discussions with Mark, they went on to create the home edition of vOUCHers. This became a small scale success and, responding to the feedback from a number of those who had bought it and, working with a number of schools, created a schools edition.

Aims of vOUCHers in school

This list shares some of our aims for using vOUCHers in school. You may well discover some further ones.

Further links to Personal Social Emotional Development (PSED) strands can be found at www.OUCHer.net.

- To develop emotional intelligence and literacy
- To identify and explore how emotions feel in the body
- To give permission that feelings and emotional language is allowed and the norm
- Validate feelings at the time
- Encourages listening without judgement or trying problem solve all the time

- Encourages talking about feelings
- Encourages children to recognise and accept the feelings and emotions in others
- To help children recognise that when there is a problem, talking can help
- Develops relationships in school
- Encourages the child to take ownership and responsibility of their emotions and feelings

List of vOUCHers

Please tick which vOUCHers you would like to use in your class.

- This voucher asks that the receiver listens to me without telling me off...
- I am having a bad day...
- This voucher asks that the receiver gives me their undivided attention to...
- This voucher asks that the receiver listens and gives me advice without telling me off...
- This voucher asks the receiver to give me their undivided attention to check my work or...
- This voucher asks the receiver to spend some time with me....
- This voucher asks the receiver to listen patiently to me. Something has happened...
- This voucher asks the receiver to listen to me. I have a problem for which I need some non-judgemental...
- I am worried about someone or something in my class...
- I am worried about someone or something at home.
- This voucher asks the receiver to tell me the truth. Someone said something, is it true?
- I have a question...
- Somebody has done something to me...
- I have been told off and I don't know why. Please can you explain it to me?
- I didn't understand something, and I am too worried to ask...
- Please can I have ______ minutes of quiet time and space, with you nearby...

How to use vOUCHers

Child displays or feels the emotion

Child acknowledges their emotions	Adult observes the child display the emotion	Child B observes Child A displaying the emotion
Child either asks for, or takes a SEC from the display (depending on the class' agreed method) and places it in front of them on the desk.	Adult provides the child with the SEC that they think is how they are feeling. Offering it with two hands	Child B either asks for, or takes, a SEC from the display (depending on the class' agreed method) and places it on the desk in front of Child A .
	SEC is incorrect and is turned over by the child to indicate this. Alternative SECs are offered until feeling is close to the SEC	SEC is incorrect and is turned over by the child to indicate this. Alternative SECs are offered by staff member or child B until feeling is close to the SEC

When appropriate, child goes to the nominated adult with their SEC. Ideally this is handed over using two hands and accepted with two hands. Using the book, the faces are then shown and the child is asked if they are feeling any of those emotions, or would they like to draw their own. Time is offered for this activity, so that the pace is slowed.

Child is asked, "Have you felt like this for long?" Allow silence and space for an answer. Then repeat back their answer to them.

Child is then asked, "And how does that feel inside your body?" Again time and space is allowed and then the words repeated back to show that the adult is actively listening

The vOUCHer is then selected. The child should be given options, based on the vOUCHers that the school has agreed to use at the child's age and stage. Specific vOUCHers, linked to their feelings should be read out to them – so that they can hear the words. Over time, the child may be able to quickly identify which vOUCHer they would like to use.

Allow the child time to choose who they would like to give their vOUCHer to and if they would like to fold it in the origami way. If the receiver is a parent or carer, consider ringing home to forewarn and advise on how to support.

Welcome to vOUCHers

For those times when you are hurting emotionally, these vOUCHers can help you find the support that you need.

Choose the vOUCHer and a person that you feel would support you best.

Then cut the vOUCHer out from this book, write yours and their name on the back. Then, either, give it to them in person or leave it somewhere that you know they will find it.

Don't be shy about asking for help. It doesn't mean you're weak, it only means you're wise.

The Japanese way of vOUCHers

Although we have no specific links with Japan, there are a few points from their culture that we would like to share that may be of help when using the vOUCHers.

Kintsukuroi is when a broken pot is repaired with gold. The repaired cracks, just like us after we have fixed our issues, can be even more precious than before. Using these vOUCHers and working our way through our tough times can help us feel more connected and special than before our issues arose.

Objects, even small ones, are given with two hands, this is to demonstrate the importance and high value of the object being given. You may wish to hand over your vOUCHer with two hands.

Origami, the Japanese art of paper folding, has been said to be a great way of helping manage stress. Engaging both the mind and hands can be very calming. Each vOUCHer has been designed to be folded into an envelope. You can follow the instructions on how to do this at www.oucher.net/voucher-folding/

How are you feeling?

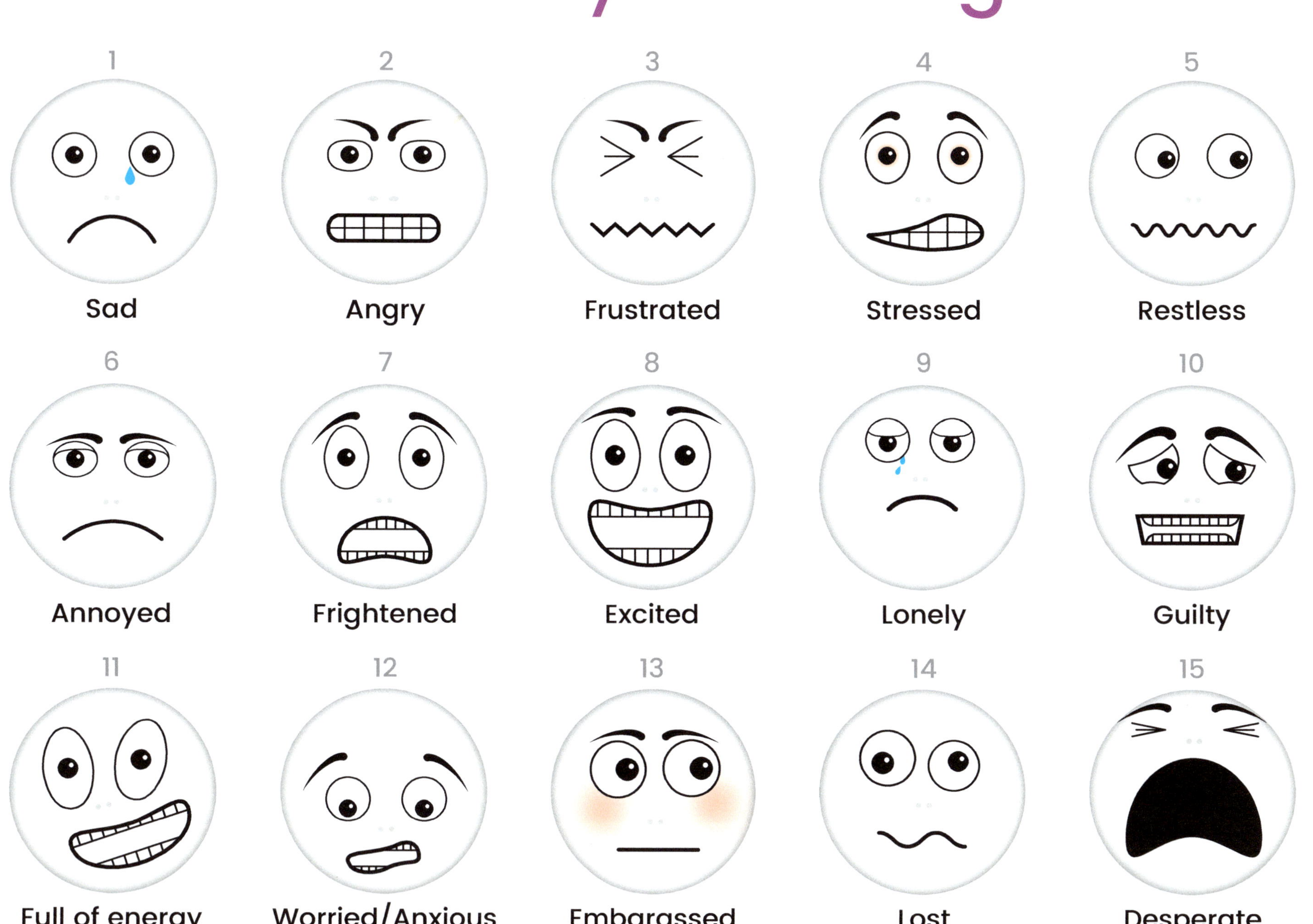

Have we missed any feelings?

If so, please draw below and label it with the emotion.

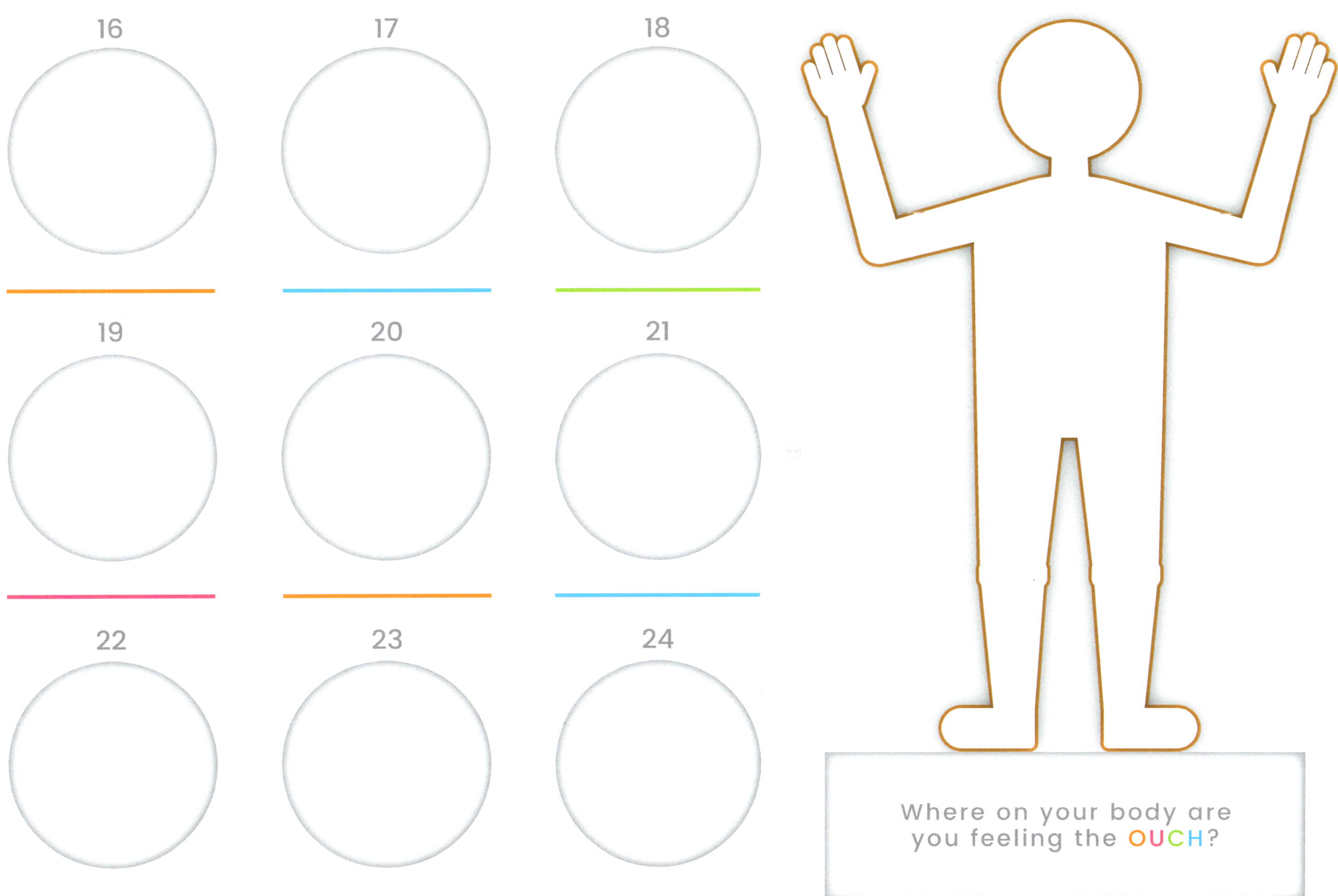

Learn more at www.OUCHer.net

A friendly listening ear

How being listened to can help

When listened to properly we can feel connected because the person has empathised with us. They really try to stand in our shoes and see the world through our eyes.

By listening and not telling you what to do leaves you with the space to discover the best option for you.

Finally, by sharing your story, feelings and thoughts you can help lift the weight off your shoulders.

A problem shared is a problem halved.

#1 Replacement password: 730172

VOUCH!

This voucher asks that the receiver listens to me without telling me off.

I did wrong, I know I did wrong and I have learned from it, but I want to tell you about it.

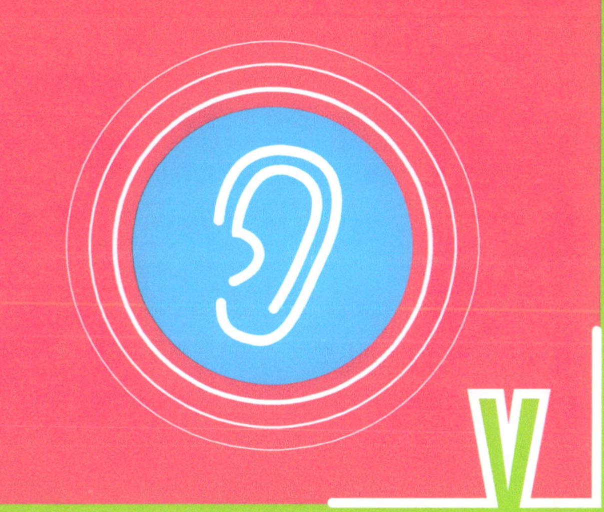

VOUCH!

This voucher asks that the receiver listens to me without telling me off.

I did wrong, I know I did wrong and I have learned from it, but I want to tell you about it.

To:
vOUCHer
From:
www.OUCHer.net

To:
vOUCHer
From:
www.OUCHer.net

Having a bad day

How letting people know how you feel can help

Sometimes others may not be able to tell if you are having a bad day and finding everything more difficult than usual.

Telling somebody you trust can help lift the weight that you may be carrying. The person you tell may also be able to help you find a new perspective on the day.

For example, a rainy day isn't a horrible day, but it is most definitely a wet day that waters flowers to enable them to grow and blossom.

It's OK to make mistakes, have bad days & be less than perfect. Do what's best for you and be yourself.

Stacie Swift

#2 Replacement password: 692691

VOUCH!

I am having a bad day.

a. Please ask me why
b. please don't ask me why I just want you to know
c. Please can we spend some time together in a quiet place

VOUCH!

I am having a bad day.

a. Please ask me why
b. Please don't ask me why I just want you to know
c. Please can we spend some time together in a quiet place

To:
vOUCHer
From:
www.OUCHer.net

To:
vOUCHer
From:
www.OUCHer.net

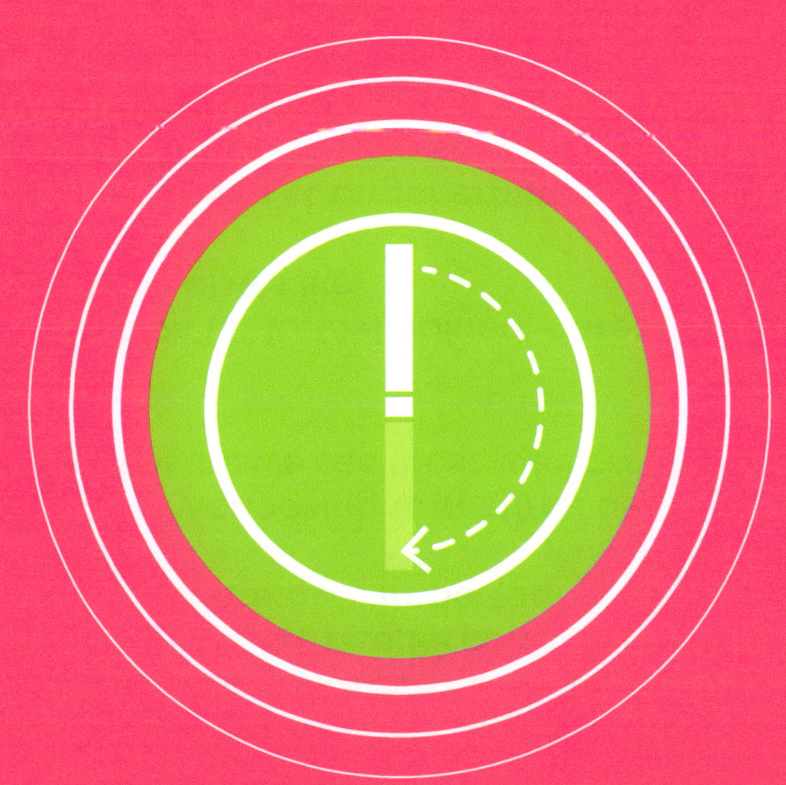

A moment of your time

How sharing a moment can help

In a world where we are busy with so many distractions like our devices, social media, tv and advertising, people can sometimes forget to prioritise the things in their life that are truly important to them.

Stopping and consciously choosing to set time aside, maybe on a regular basis, to connect and ensure we see those we care about most is of benefit to both parties.

Sharing a moment helps us to feel valued, cared for and that we are a special part of someone else's life.

Memories that are linked with stronger emotions are easier to remember which is why we can remember those special times and big events in our lives though may not be able to remember what we did last Tuesday.

Time is the most valuable thing a person can spend.

Theophrastus

#3 Replacement password: 468265

VOUCH!

This voucher asks that the receiver gives me their undivided attention to:

a. Talk with me about my day, it's been ____________________

b. Listen to me talk about my day without comment or judgement, it's been ____________________

c. Sit with me, I just need you to be near

d. Tell me about your day

VOUCH!

This voucher asks that the receiver gives me their undivided attention to:

a. Talk with me about my day, it's been ____________________

b. Listen to me talk about my day without comment or judgement, it's been ____________________

c. Sit with me, I just need you to be near

d. Tell me about your day

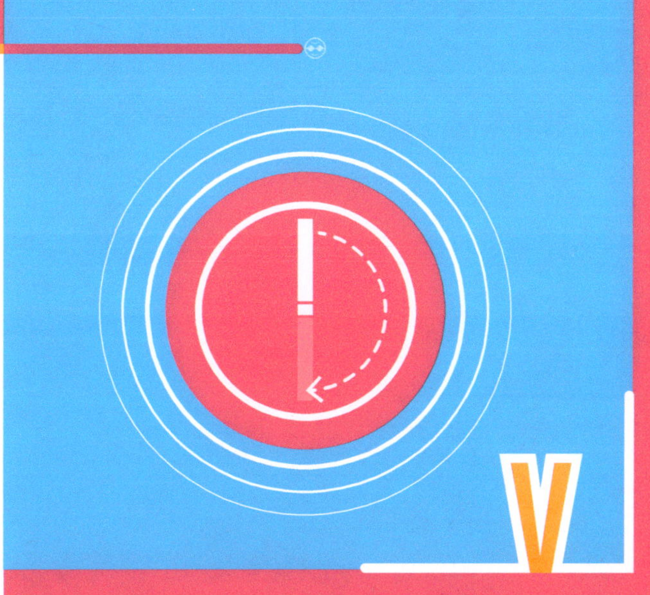

To:
vOUCHer
From:
www.OUCHer.net

To:
vOUCHer
From:
www.OUCHer.net

Listen then speak

How listening to advice can help

Sometimes when we are anxious, stressed or feeling down, the emotions can make it difficult to think clearly and logically.

Scientists at the University of Pittsburgh discovered that negative emotions like anxiety can hinder us in making the best choices for our lives.

Seeking advice from someone you trust can help you think more clearly. It may also help you to find your own solutions.

Remember, it is your life and you can choose whether or not to take the advice you are given.

All the advice in the world will never help you until you help yourself

Fred Van Amburgh

#4 Replacement password: 210836

VOUCH!

This voucher asks that the receiver listens and gives me advice without telling me off or getting angry about what I am going to say.

VOUCH!

This voucher asks that the receiver listens and gives me advice without telling me off or getting angry about what I am going to say.

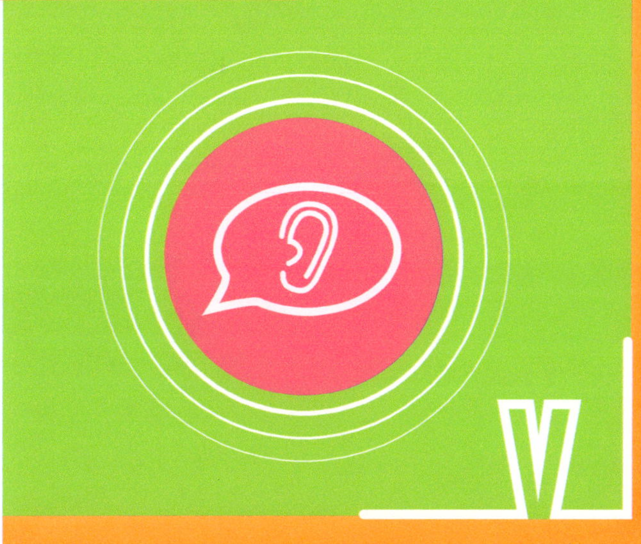

To:
vOUCHer
From:
www.OUCHer.net

To:
vOUCHer
From:
www.OUCHer.net

Undivided Attention

How being given undivided attention can help

Having the undivided attention of someone else is powerful because it shows that you are cared about.

We can lack focus with screens, people and problems all vying for our attention.

When we consciously choose to give somebody our full attention, a real connection can happen that can help both the giver and receiver feel calmer and less stressed.

The greatest gift you can give anyone is your undivided attention.

Will Schwalbe

#5 Replacement password: 967120

VOUCH!

This voucher asks the receiver to give me their undivided attention to:

a. Check my work
b. Have a drink and chat
c. Read together
d. Play a game or do puzzles

VOUCH!

This voucher asks the receiver to give me their undivided attention to:

a. Check my work
b. Have a drink and chat
c. Read together
d. Play a game or do puzzles

To:
vOUCHer
From:
www.OUCHer.net

To:
vOUCHer
From:
www.OUCHer.net

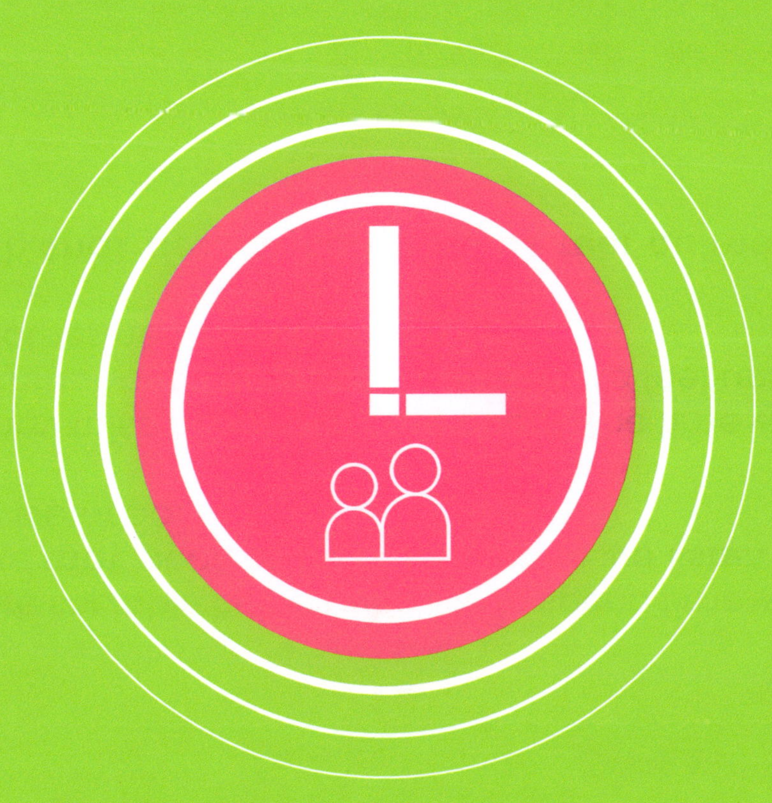

Spend time together

How spending time together can help

As humans, we are sociable beings who like to spend time with other people. At other times we may need to be alone. When we listen to ourselves we know which one we need.

Sometimes we may miss people we care about. The time we spend without them can be painful. These times can cause us to feel unsettled, nervous, distressed or another negative emotion.

Connecting with that person can help us feel calmer and increase our confidence.

Spending time with you is so precious and I love every minute that we are together.

#6 Replacement password: 104729

VOUCH!

This voucher asks the receiver to spend some time with me.

I have drawn how I am feeling

VOUCH!

This voucher asks the receiver to spend some time with me.

I have drawn how I am feeling

To:
vOUCHer
From:
www.OUCHer.net

To:
vOUCHer
From:
www.OUCHer.net

Be Patient

How being patient can help

By being shown patience and space we can give ourselves the opportunity to find our own solutions.

Sounds, movement, thoughts and emotions all create energy waves, but for any wave to be generated it needs space. Imagine a butterfly in a cacoon trying to fly. There would be no space for it to take flight.

What patience can give us is the space to allow thoughts and feeling to fulfil their purpose of being thought and felt. Patience can help us remove the cocoon and to spread our wings for us to move towards our full potential.

Have patience. All things are difficult before they become easy.

Saadi

#7 Replacement password: 658302

VOUCH!

This voucher asks the receiver to listen patiently to me. Something has happened that has made me feel:

I have drawn how I am feeling

VOUCH!

This voucher asks the receiver to listen patiently to me. Something has happened that has made me feel:

I have drawn how I am feeling

To:
vOUCHer
From:
www.OUCHer.net

To:
vOUCHer
From:
www.OUCHer.net

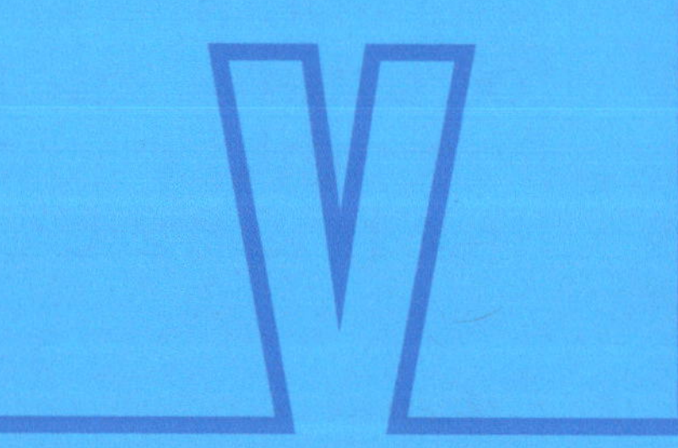

Speak without judgement

How non-judgement can help

Nobody has spent their whole lives with another person, except us with ourselves. Even as babies we had our own unique thoughts, feelings, experiences and perspectives whilst being born and sleeping alone at night.

For this reason, it is said that we can never know enough to judge another person. It is impossible to know what each person has fully experienced in their whole life and why someone may have behaved the way they did.

When a person is not judged they can feel accepted for who they truly are. Instead of being judged and labelled, they can feel that the person they are speaking to is coming from a place of empathy and compassion in trying to understand the situation from their point of view.

Be curious, not judgmental.

Walt Whitman

#8 Replacement password: 079183

VOUCH!

This voucher asks the receiver to listen to me. I have a problem for which I need some non-judgemental advice based on what you might do if you were in my position.

I have drawn how I am feeling

VOUCH!

This voucher asks the receiver to listen to me. I have a problem for which I need some non-judgemental advice based on what you might do if you were in my position.

I have drawn how I am feeling

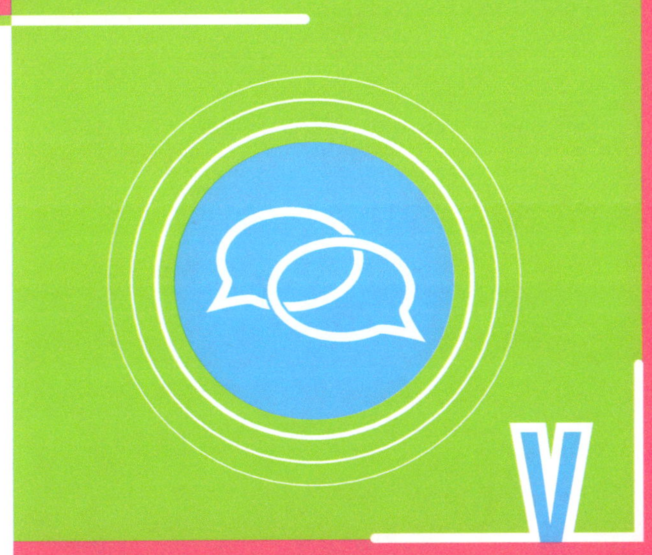

To:
vOUCHer
From:
www.OUCHer.net

To:
vOUCHer
From:
www.OUCHer.net

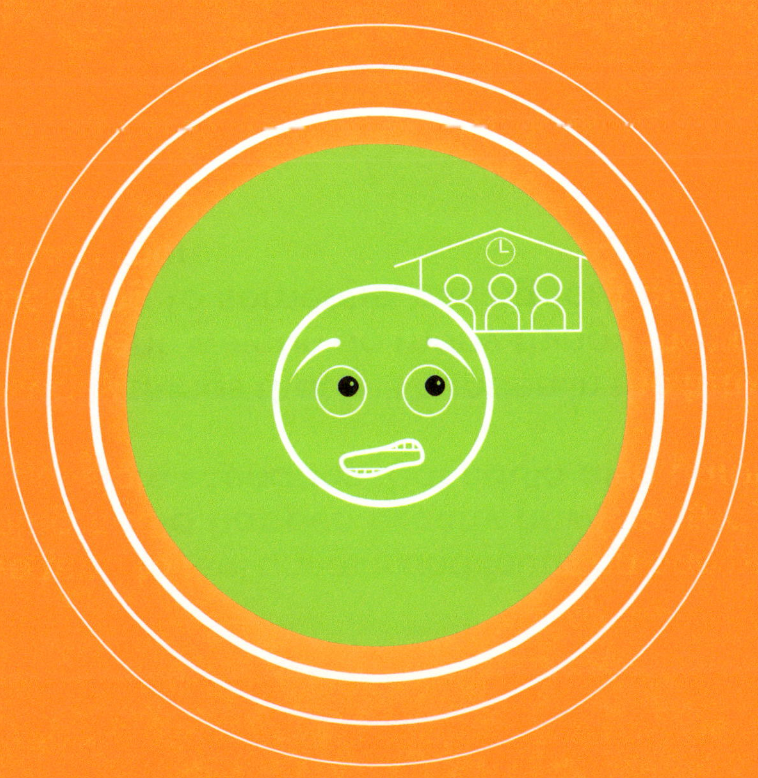

School Worry

How taking action can help

When we worry we tend to feel uneasy and focus on one possible outcome. Although everything could happen exactly how we imagine it, there are also many other possible scenarios that could also unfold.

Our worries are usually things that will happen in the future. Meaning that right now, in this moment, we can do many things that may help change the future. Like speaking to someone, asking for help, changing the way we behave and much more.

Do what you can, with what you have, where you are.

Theodore Roosevelt

#9 Replacement password: 452769

VOUCH!

I am worried about someone or something in my class.

a. Please talk to me about it

b. Please call ________________ about it

c. Please don't ask me about it, I just want you to know

VOUCH!

I am worried about someone or something in my class.

a. Please talk to me about it

b. Please call ________________ about it

c. Please don't ask me about it, I just want you to know

To:
vOUCHer
From:
www.OUCHer.net

To:
vOUCHer
From:
www.OUCHer.net

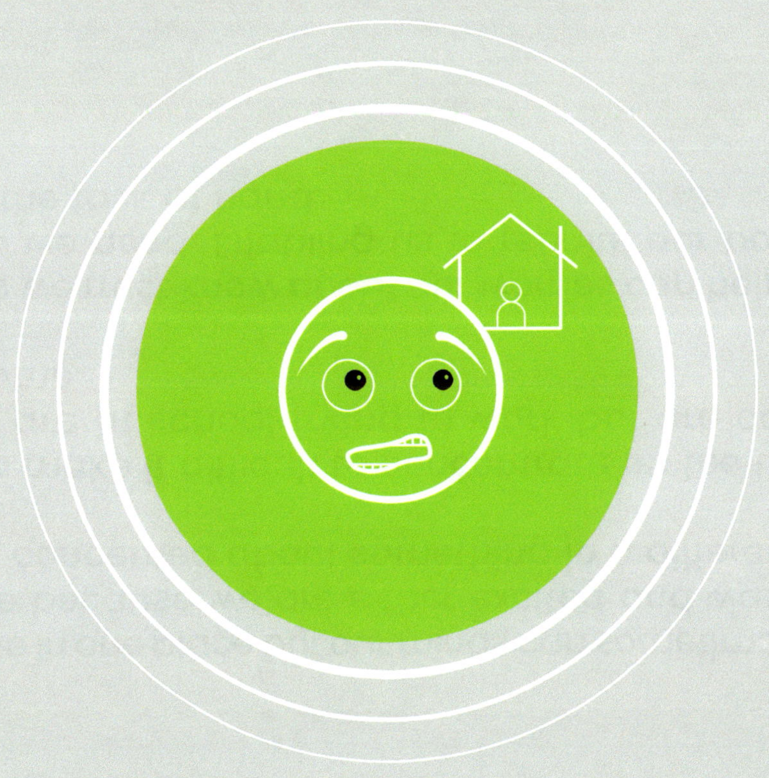

Home Worry

How home worry help

Our bodies can be in one place but our minds can sometimes be somewhere else. This can be because we are either excited and want to be there or are worried and concerned about something in a different place.

These times can make it difficult to concentrate on the task at hand. For example, if you are at school trying to work but are concerned about something at home.

Letting someone we trust know about our worries can help us get the help and perspective we need. Enabling us to reunite our body and mind to concentrate on the task at hand.

A distraction doesn’t pull you away from your primary goal, but it reveals your true desires.

Unknown

#10 Replacement password: 298375

VOUCH!

I am worried about someone or something at home.

a. Please talk to me about it

b. Please call ________________ about it

c. Please don't ask me about it, I just want you to know

VOUCH!

I am worried about someone or something at home.

a. Please talk to me about it

b. Please call ________________ about it

c. Please don't ask me about it, I just want you to know

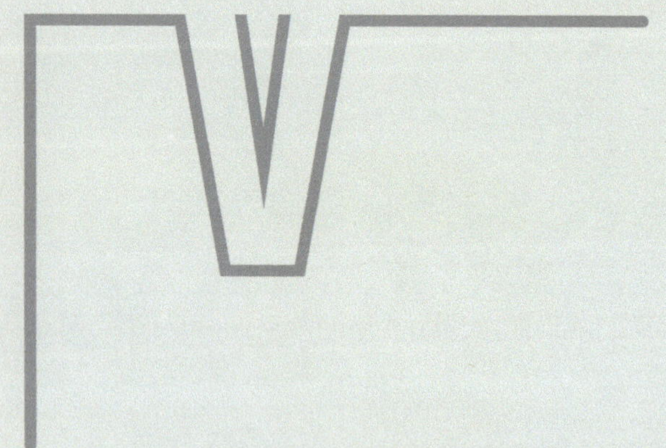

To:
vOUCHer
From:
www.OUCHer.net

To:
vOUCHer
From:
www.OUCHer.net

Clarifying

How clarifying can help

Getting more than one opinion before deciding your own view can help you have peace of mind. Knowing that you have heard a broad range of views can help you feel more confident about your decision.

Understanding your own views can help you develop your next step by giving you the purpose, courage and confidence to do so.

Clarifying also demonstrates maturity, by realising that different views can help you extend your knowledge to make an informed choice that is best for you.

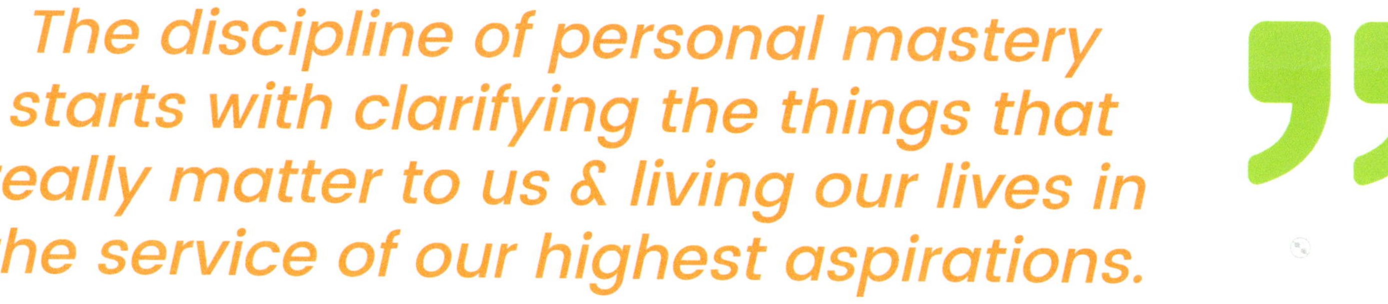

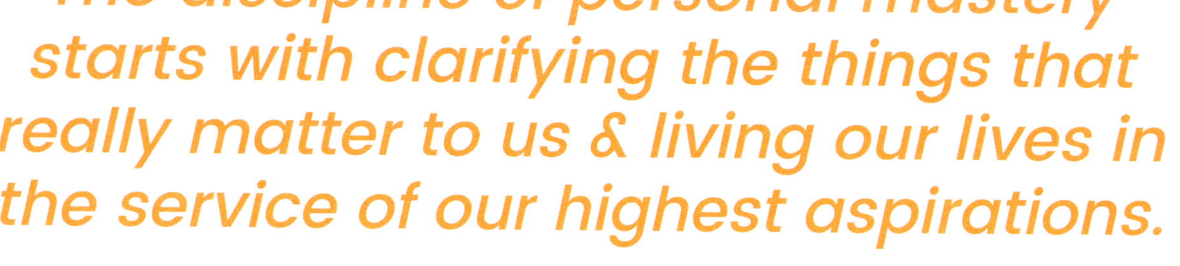

The discipline of personal mastery starts with clarifying the things that really matter to us & living our lives in the service of our highest aspirations.

Peter Senge

#11 Replacement password: 128794

VOUCH!

This voucher asks the receiver to tell me the truth. Someone said: ______________________

____

____

Is this true?

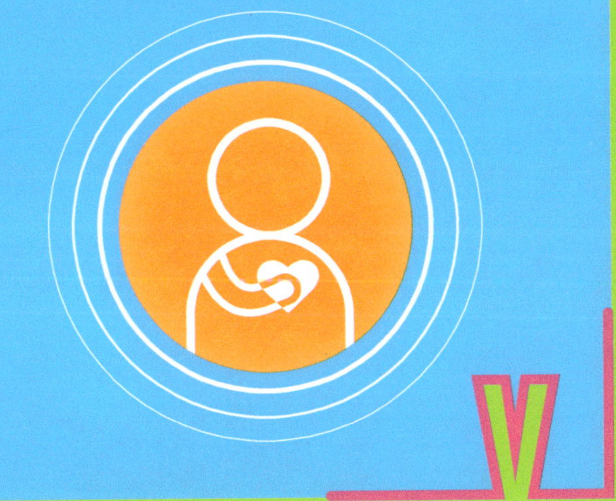

VOUCH!

This voucher asks the receiver to tell me the truth. Someone said: ______________________

____

____

Is this true?

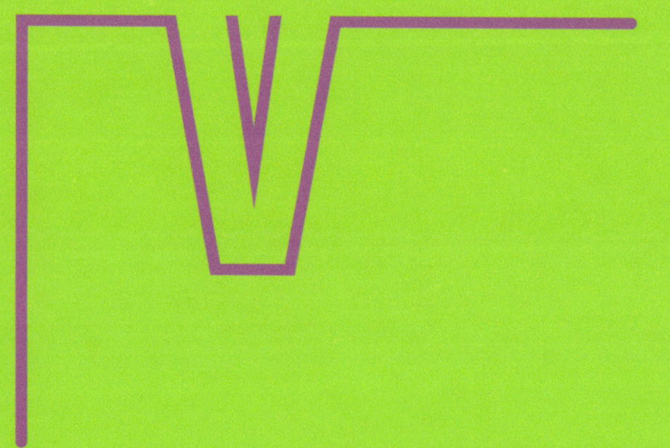

To:
vOUCHer
From:
www.OUCHer.net

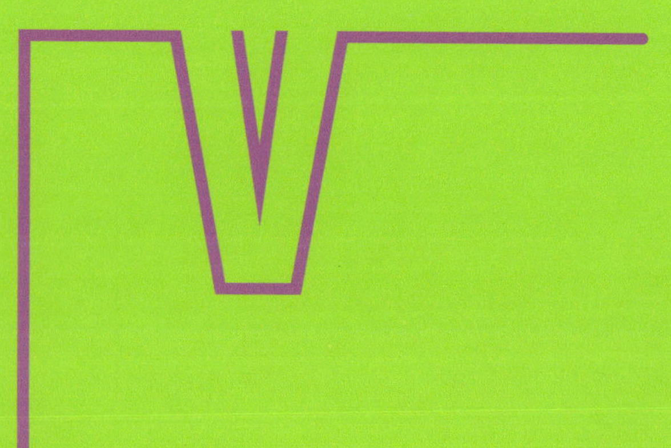

To:
vOUCHer
From:
www.OUCHer.net

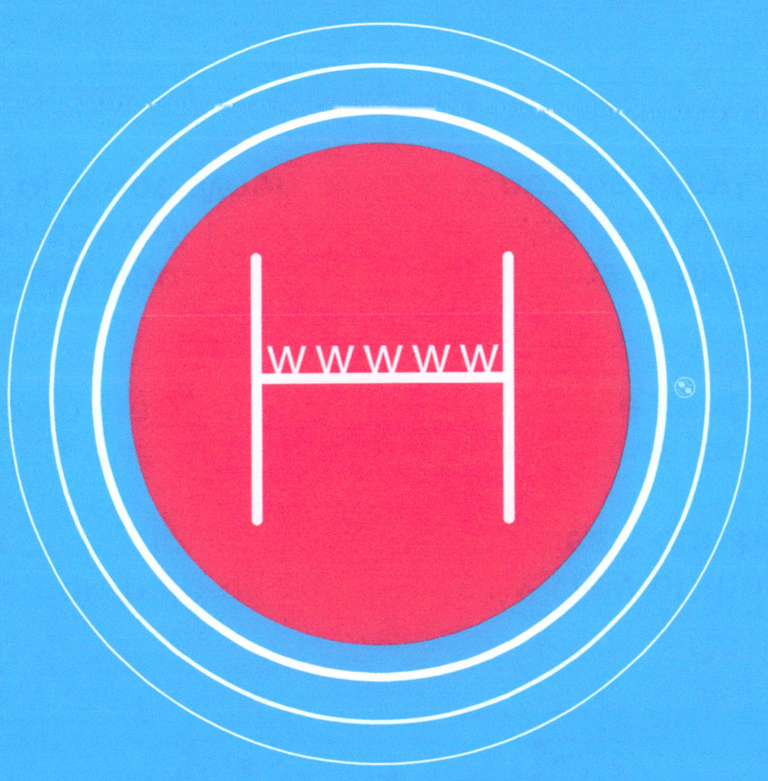

I have a question

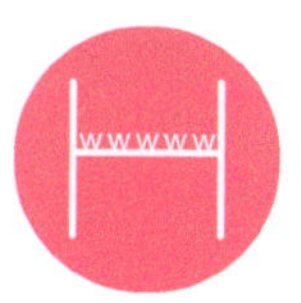

How questioning can help

Asking questions can help us to find a new view of the world. This can support us in life and help us with the difficulties it can bring.

Finding and asking questions of other people can be a fantastic way to expand our own understanding, knowledge and views on many different topics.

If you are wondering what to ask, remember the 5 birds sat on a rugby post (see the icon above). The H shaped rugby post is the **How** and the 5 birds are the W's of **What**, **When**, **Where**, **Who** and **Why**!

Even though there are no ways of knowing for sure, there are ways of knowing for pretty sure.

Lemony Snicket

#12 Replacement password: 072945

VOUCH!

I have a question: ______________________

____

____

____

____

VOUCH!

I have a question: ______________________

____

____

____

____

To:
vOUCHer
From:
www.OUCHer.net

To:
vOUCHer
From:
www.OUCHer.net

Something's happened to me

How getting support can help

When stuck and in need of support at school, we put up our hands and get the help we require to continue.

This is the same for life. For most things that happen in life, we can cope and deal with them. However occasionally someone does something to us that we can not handle. Leaving us needing help and support.

Asking for that help and support can be scary but so can doing nothing and letting the situation happen again. This can leave us feeling conflicted as to what to do.

By realising that choosing to share our situation and feelings with a trusted adult is one way we can begin to change what is happening to us.

Ask for help. Not because you are weak. But because you want to remain strong.

Les Brown

#12 Replacement password: 987653

VOUCH!

Somebody has done something to me.

a. I want to tell you about it
b. I don't want to tell you about it
c. Can we spend some time together in a quiet place?

I have drawn how I am feeling

VOUCH!

Somebody has done something to me.

a. I want to tell you about it
b. I don't want to tell you about it
c. Can we spend some time together in a quiet place?

I have drawn how I am feeling

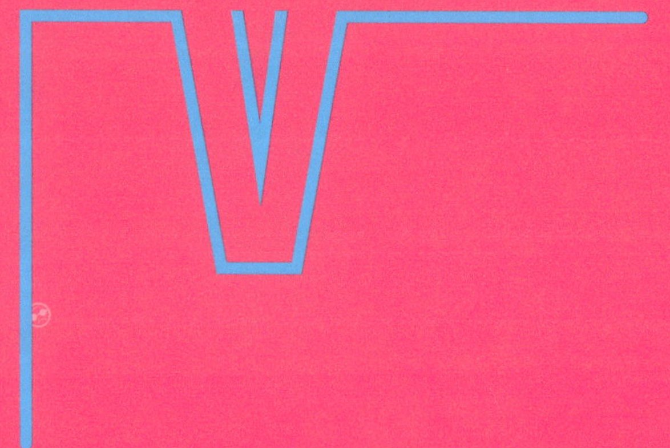

To:
vOUCHer
From:
www.OUCHer.net

To:
vOUCHer
From:
www.OUCHer.net

Please explain

How asking questions can help

We all know when something feels unfair. If a trusted adult had 10 sweets to give to 2 children. The first child received 7 sweets and the second child was only given 3. There would be a feeling of injustice and the second child may well ask why they received 4 less than the first child.

The answers to our questions around unfairness can help us understand why something happened. It could be a mistake by the grown-ups or there could be a good reason that may help us understand why.

However, it is better to know what happened than to be left feeling hurt.

Life is unfair.
And it's not fair
that life is unfair.

Edward Abbey

#12 Replacement password: 985476

VOUCH!

I have been told off and I don't know why.

Please can you explain it to me?

VOUCH!

I have been told off and I don't know why.

Please can you explain it to me?

To:
vOUCHer
From:
www.OUCHer.net

To:
vOUCHer
From:
www.OUCHer.net

Not understanding

How understanding can help

Even the most intelligent people in the world do not know the answer to every question. For example, if we asked the cleverest person in the world for the first and surname of your school's headteacher they will more than likely not know.

However, when clever people do not know or understand something they will try and discover the answer for themselves by reading books or searching the internet. Then if they still cannot find the answer they will ask people who they think will be able to give them the answer.

Sometimes it can be scary to ask questions. In schools, it's the grown-ups job to help students understand. They would much prefer you ask instead of worrying about not knowing the answer.

> *Don't be afraid to ask questions. Don't be afraid to ask for help when you need it. I do that every day. Asking for help isn't a sign of weakness, it's a sign of strength. It shows you have the courage to admit when you don't know something, and to learn something new.*
>
> Barack Obama - 44th President of the United States

#13 Replacement password: 527392

VOUCH!

I didn't understand something, and I am too worried to ask.

VOUCH!

I didn't understand something, and I am too worried to ask.

To:
vOUCHer
From:
www.OUCHer.net

To:
vOUCHer
From:
www.OUCHer.net

Quiet time and space

How being quiet can help

Taking time to be quiet and sit in silence can give us space to find the answers we are looking for.

Because our thoughts and feelings can sometimes be like clothes spinning round and round in a tumble dryer. Taking the time to contemplate what we are going through can give our thoughts and feelings the opportunity to fulfil their purpose of being thought and felt. Thus allowing us the possibility of a new perspective to move forward with more certainty.

Your mind will answer most questions if you learn to relax and wait for the answer.

William S. Burroughs

#12 Replacement password: 987653

VOUCH!

Please can I have ______ minutes of quiet time and space, with you nearby.

a. I need it, please ask me why

b. I need it, please don't ask me why

c. I need it, I want to tell you why, but I don't yet have the words to tell you yet

VOUCH!

Please can I have ______ minutes of quiet time and space, with you nearby.

a. I need it, please ask me why

b. I need it, please don't ask me why

c. I need it, I want to tell you why, but I don't yet have the words to tell you yet

To:
vOUCHer
From:
www.OUCHer.net

To:
vOUCHer
From:
www.OUCHer.net

Learn more at www.OUCHer.net

Additional support

For those times you are unsure who to speak to, there are organisations that can offer you support, should you wish to contact them.

Samaritans

If you need someone to talk to, we listen. We won't judge or tell you what to do.

116123

jo@samaritans.org

www.samaritans.org

childline

ONLINE, ON THE PHONE, ANYTIME

Childline

A free, private and confidential service where you can talk about anything.

0800 1111

www.childline.org.uk

Kooth

Free, safe and anonymous online support for young people. Kooth can be someone to understand or to offer advice when you need it.

www.kooth.com

Shout

24/7 UK crisis text service available for times when people feel they need immediate support.

www.giveusashout.org

Text 85258

Young Minds

Leading the fight for a future where all young minds are supported and empowered, whatever the challenges.

0808 802 5544

www.youngminds.org.uk

Calm Harm

Calm Harm is an app developed for teenage mental health charity stem4 by Dr Nihara Krause it uses an evidence-based therapy called Dialectical Behavioural Therapy (DBT).

www.calmharm.co.uk

Crisis

Crisis is the UK national charity for homeless people. The charity offers year-round education, employment, housing and well-being serviceshomeless.

www.crisis.org.uk

LGBT Foundation

LGBT Foundation is a national charity delivering advice, support and information services to lesbian, gay, bisexual & trans communities.

0345 3 30 30 30

www.lgbt.foundation

Mindfulness NHS

Paying more attention to the present moment – to your own thoughts and feelings, and to the world around you – can improve your mental wellbeing. You can check your mood using this simple mood self-assessment quiz.

www.nhs.uk/conditions/stress-anxiety-depression/mindfulness/

About the creators of vOUCHers

Jennifer Dunning

Having initially worked in the care sector supporting children, Jennifer now works in education with a particular interest in special educational needs.

From both at work and volunteering with Samaritans, Jennifer is acutely aware of the impact trauma and emotional turmoil can have on everyday life. Jennifer believes that by developing a network of support and talking about these issues we can move towards feeling and ultimately easing our difficult emotions.

Markus Baker

With his first career as a nursery nurse along with Markus' current one as a visual communicator creates a perfect mix for unique ideas to come to life.

Markus has a broad view of society. This comes from his many experiences that include designing for the film industry, volunteering for Samaritans, qualifying as a psychotherapist and travelling the world, which included staying with a Taoist Master in the hills of South Korea.

Did you spot Sam hiding on every page and vOUCHer in this book? If you didn't it is ok because Sam was not supposed to found until you were aware.

Look at Sam's face and tilt your head to your right and then tilt your head to the left. It is the same face but one looks happy and from the other angle it looks sad.

Sam's face represents that sometimes a situation does not change, but how we see it does.

Each of the vOUCHers and pages in this book can help you develop a different view and way of looking at your life.

Jennifer and Markus hope you enjoyed this book and that you found it helpful. If you would like to tell us what you think about this book, please do so at www.OUCHer.net

MORE BOOKS BY R&Q

www.ingramcontent.com/pod-product-compliance
Lightning Source LLC
LaVergne TN
LVHW070139110826
845147LV00002B/290
9781916357150